What Is a GOVERNMENT?

By Logan Everett
and Simon Adams

CELEBRATION PRESS
Pearson Learning Group

The following people from **Pearson Learning Group**
have contributed to the development of this product:

Joan Mazzeo, Dorothea Fox **Design**	**Editorial** Leslie Feierstone Barna, Teri Crawford Jones
Christine Fleming **Marketing**	**Publishing Operations** Jennifer Van Der Heide

Production Laura Benford-Sullivan

Content Area Consultants Dr. Daniel J. Gelo

The following people from **DK** have
contributed to the development of this product:

Art Director Rachael Foster

Martin Wilson **Managing Art Editor**	**Managing Editor** Marie Greenwood
Kath Northam **Design**	**Editorial** Marian Broderick
Sarah Duncan, Pernilla Pearce **Picture Research**	**Production** Gordana Simakovic
Richard Czapnik, Andy Smith **Cover Design**	**DTP** David McDonald

Consultant Simon Adams

Dorling Kindersley would like to thank: Sarah Crouch for preliminary design work; Lucy Heaver for editorial research; Mariana Sonnenburg and Carlo Ortu for additional picture research; Johnny Pau for additional cover design work; and Hannah Wilson.

Photographs: Every effort has been made to secure permission and provide appropriate credit for photographic material. The publisher deeply regrets any omission and pledges to correct errors called to its attention in subsequent editions.

Unless otherwise acknowledged, all photographs are the property of Dorling Kindersley.

Photo locators denoted as follows: Top (T), Center (C), Bottom (B), Left (L), Right (R), Background (Bkgd)

Picture Credits: CVR(CL) klikk/Fotolia; **CVR(CR)** Monika Wisniewska/Shutterstock; **CVR(T)** Monkey Business Images/Shutterstock; **CVR(B)** Jake Lyell/Alamy; **001B** Tyler Olson/Fotolia; **001BC** Marcito/Fotolia; **001C** Jan Kratochvila/Shutterstock; **001CL** Horia Bogdan/Shutterstock; **001CR** Vacclav/Fotolia; **001TL** Photocreo/Fotolia; **003** jStock/Fotolia; **006B** James Frank/Alamy; **006C** Ton Koene/Horizons WWP/Alamy; **006T** Rafael Ben-Ari/Fotolia; **007B** Lisa F. Young/Fotolia; **007T** Junial Enterprises/Fotolia; **008B** erikdegraaf/Fotolia; **008C** byrdyak/Fotolia; **008T** Craig Holmes Premium/Alamy; **009B** Esbobeldijk/Fotolia; **009C** Sayyid Azim/AP Images; **009T** Gary Blakeley/Fotolia; **010B** Z1009/_Jan-Peter Kasper/dpa/picture-alliance/Newscom; **010T** Jacky Chapman/Alamy; **011** Dudarev Mikhail/Fotolia; **012B** INTERFOTO/Alamy; **012C** anastasios71/Fotolia; **012T** akg-images/Newscom; **013B** claudiozacc/Fotolia; **013T** Goran Bogicevic/Fotolia; **014T** World History Archive/Alamy; **015B** Photo12 Collection/Alamy; **015C** Christopher Hurst/The National Trust Photolibrary/Alamy; **015T** Alistair Laming/Alamy; **017CL** Luc Novovitch/Alamy; **017BL** Paul A. Souders/Corbis; **017BR** Peter Turnley/Corbis; **017CR** Stephanie Maze/Corbis; **017T** Michael Flippo/Fotolia; **018B** Photocreo/Fotolia; **018C** Trevor Collens/Alamy; **018T** John Stillwell/PA WIRE/EPA/Newscom; **019B** Bill Ingalls/NASA; **019T** David Brauchli/AP Images; **020B** Peter Probst/Alamy; **020T** Julio Etchart/Alamy; **021B** David Longstreath/AP Images; **021T** Tim Rooke/Rex Features/Presselect/Alamy; **022** Jonathan Noden-Wilkinson/Shutterstock; **023B** Aldo Liverani/Andia/Alamy; **023T** Richard Vogel/AP Images; **024BL** NIC BOTHMA/EPA/Newscom; **024BR** AMIT BHARGAVA/AP Images; **024T** Everett Collection Historical/Alamy; **025L** Andres Leighton/AP Images; **025R** ANTONIO AMARAL/EPA/Newscom; **026** Jandke/Caro/Alamy; **027B** INTERFOTO/Alamy; **027T** akg-images/Newscom; **028T** Xalanx/Fotolia; **029B** ANDY JATMIKO/AP Images; **029T** CARLO FERRARO/AFP/Newscom

All other images: 🖾 Dorling Kindersley © 2005. For further information see www.dkimages.com

ISBN: 0-7652-5250-3

Color reproduction by Colourscan, Singapore
Printed in Mexico
26   16

Contents

What Do Governments Do?

A government is a system that helps people live and work together in a local community or in a nation.

Governments do this in different ways. For example, governments make laws and run the armed services and police departments to protect people. They provide services such as transportation, education, and healthcare to help people in their daily lives. They look after the environment to protect the planet we live on.

Money systems enable people to buy and sell goods and services.

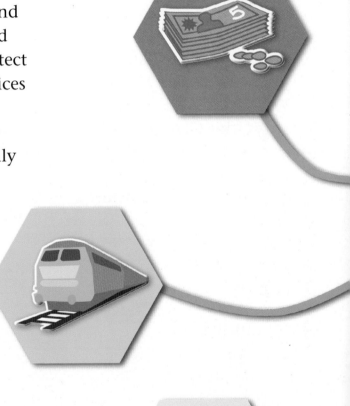

Transportation systems make it possible for people to move from place to place easily.

Environmental policy helps to protect the planet and natural resources.

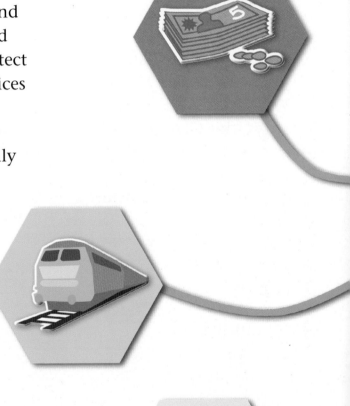

Laws are developed to keep order.

Military forces protect a country from invasion.

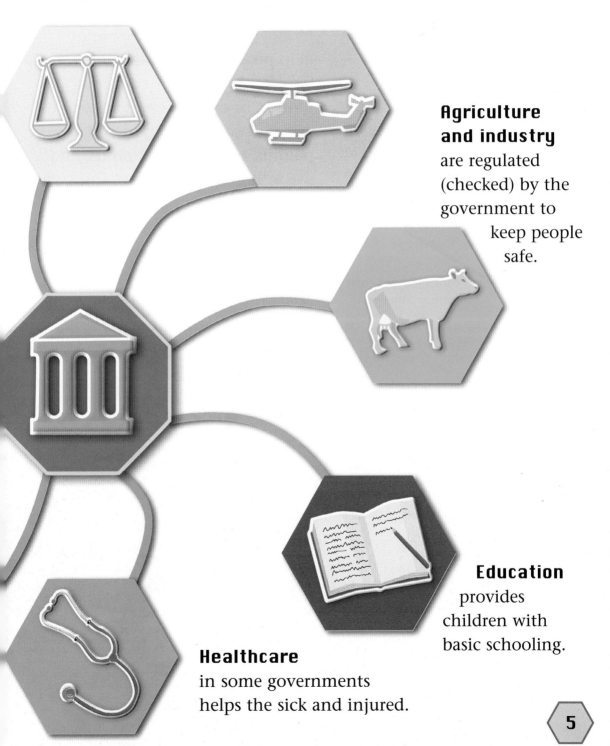

Agriculture and industry are regulated (checked) by the government to keep people safe.

Education provides children with basic schooling.

Healthcare in some governments helps the sick and injured.

Money Systems

The government in each country organizes that country's money system. Money systems help people buy and sell goods and services. In different countries, money, or **currency**, is called different names, such as dollars, pounds, euros, rupees, rands, and pesos. Both paper money and coins are produced, or minted, by the government. The money is produced in the United Kingdom's Royal Mint, the U.S. Mint, or the Royal Australian Mint in Canberra.

banknotes and coins from around the world

Education

Every child has the right to an education. Education helps children learn to read, write, and calculate. Education also helps children learn about the world and its people. Most governments help to educate their citizens by providing schools, colleges, and universities. They also provide libraries, sports centers, art galleries, and computer centers.

Somali children in school

children in school in China

Laws

One of the main responsibilities of any government is to develop and pass laws. Laws are designed to keep people safe and healthy, and protect the environment. The first step is for **citizens** and their representatives to recognize there is a problem and that a new law needs to be made. The process of having a new law adopted can take months or sometimes years.

a judge in the United States

Healthcare

Many governments have a very important role in making sure people are healthy. In some countries, they pay doctors to visit people when they are ill and provide hospitals to care for people who are sick or need to have an operation. Some countries provide training for doctors and nurses. A government may also run emergency services, such as ambulance corps.

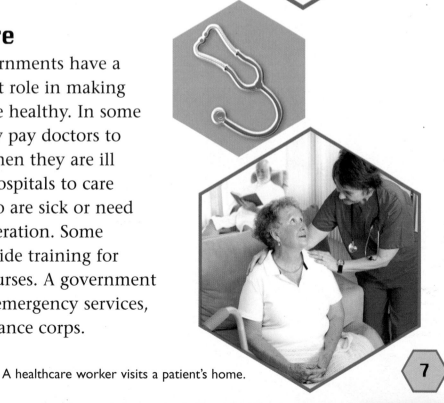

A healthcare worker visits a patient's home.

Transportation Systems

People need transportation for both work and pleasure. Many governments provide transportation systems, such as roads, railways, ports, and airports. Some of these are run by governments, while others are run by private companies. Most importantly, governments make sure the cars, buses, trains, boats, and planes in use are safe for travel.

Spaghetti Junction, Birmingham, United Kingdom

sheep farm in the United States

Agriculture and Industry

Farms provide us with the food we eat. Governments help farmers protect the land they farm and work with them to develop new crops and better methods of farming. Governments assist with the export of food and livestock to other countries. They also ensure that all food is safe to eat and that all farm animals are healthy.

tea harvest in India

Military Forces

The first duty of every national government is to protect its country from invasion by an enemy. Most governments do this by paying for and providing armed services, such as an army, a navy, and an air force. Many armed services provide assistance to their citizens and the country's neighbors in times of need. Governments also train young men and women to serve in these forces.

Canadian air force

Kenyan army inspection

wind farm in New Zealand

Environmental Policy

Most people are very concerned about the state of the planet and the damage people are doing to it. Many governments help the environment by encouraging people to recycle paper and other items, and to conserve energy and water. They also help prevent pollution and protect the rivers, streams, and lakes from suffering too much damage.

Early Governments

Governments developed in different places at different times. Just as people have different histories, cultures, and expectations, so do their governments. From the earliest times, people have created governments to meet their needs and to look after themselves, their families, and their communities.

prehistoric cave painting in Zimbabwe

The First Governments

For thousands of years, people didn't need governments. Humans lived in small groups, usually made up of families or relatives. Everyone shared the work, and everyone talked together to solve problems. These groups might have had a leader who took control in times of danger, but most decisions would have been made by the whole group.

As time went by, people started to grow more food. Because of the development of permanent agriculture, people settled near their fields. Slowly, these settlements grew into larger communities.

This 3,300-year-old clay map of an ancient Mesopotamian city (in present-day Iraq) shows irrigation systems, roads, and public buildings. This city must have had a government to organize these works.

The benefits of being part of a large group included safety in numbers and having a large workforce for building or farming projects. As the groups grew larger, the need for organized government became greater. In some communities, leaders were granted power by their people. In other places, a powerful person seized control of the community. Whatever the form of government, the leaders developed laws that the people had to follow. Some rulers were fair and kind to the people, but sometimes the people were taxed heavily or enslaved.

Ancient Egypt

For centuries, the people of ancient Egypt, who lived alongside the Nile River, were ruled by dynasties, or families, of rulers known as pharaohs. When one pharaoh died, his son or brother, or sometimes his wife or daughter, became the next ruler. Ancient Egyptians believed that the pharaohs were not ordinary humans, but were divine, or gods in their own right. Pharaohs lived in great luxury. They had the power of life and death over their subjects. Pharaohs built pyramids as their final resting place.

Pharaoh Khufu of Egypt (2551–2528 B.C.) used local workers, and sometimes slaves, to build the Great Pyramid (center).

Ancient Greece

Ancient Greece was made up of many small city-states, such as Athens, Sparta, and Thebes. There was no single ruler over the city-states. Each city-state had a different government system.

Almost 3,000 years ago, a form of government called **democracy** (from two Greek words meaning "people" and "rule") was invented in the city-state of Athens. In a democracy, all citizens were allowed to take part in making decisions. Citizens voted on all decisions. They took turns serving on a council that developed laws. They served on juries to decide whether or not someone had broken the law.

This democracy wasn't perfect. Not everyone in Athens was considered a citizen. Women and slaves couldn't take part in the government. Citizens didn't always have enough information to make careful decisions. However, the democracy in Athens was successful for many years. It also inspired many present-day governments.

Pericles was a champion of democracy in ancient Greece. He built the Parthenon, a famous temple.

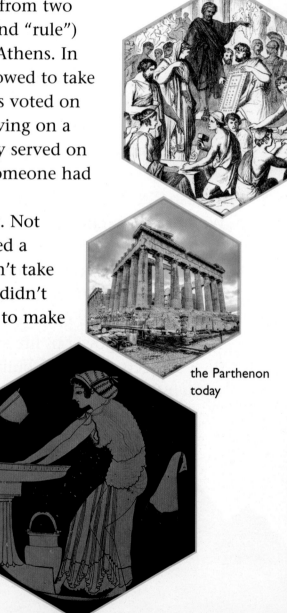

the Parthenon today

A rich woman is shown washing on a fourth-century-B.C. vase. Even wealthy women were not allowed to vote in ancient Greece.

Ancient Rome

Claudius was a strong emperor who ruled from A.D. 41 to 54.

The city of Rome was founded in 753 B.C. At first, Rome was a **monarchy** governed by kings. Many of these kings did illegal things and ordered people to do things they didn't always want to do. In 509 B.C. the monarchy was overthrown and Rome became a **republic**. Two consuls, or leaders, ran the republic. One was a wealthy member of the upper class and the other was a member of the working class.

The Roman republic lasted until 27 B.C., when one consul, named Augustus, seized power and became the first Roman emperor. He had absolute power over every citizen in the Roman Empire, which soon stretched across most of Europe and North Africa. The Roman consuls and emperors all took advice from the Senate, which was the main lawmaking institution in Rome, just like the Senate is in the United States today.

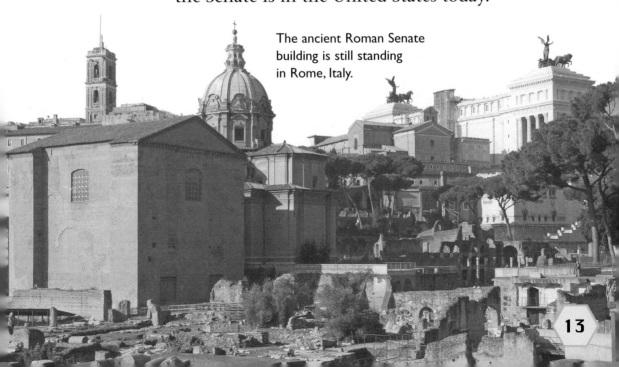

The ancient Roman Senate building is still standing in Rome, Italy.

Rulers Around the World

Ancient Egypt was ruled by pharaohs who thought they were gods, while Ancient Greece was governed by its own citizens. Historically, however, most countries have followed Ancient Rome and have been ruled by a monarch. These monarchs have had different names. Some were called emperors or kings and queens, while others have been called sultans or tsars.

Sulayman I ruled the Ottoman Empire from 1520 to 1566. He had complete power, but was a fair ruler. He was known as Sulayman the Lawgiver.

Generally, monarchs inherited their title because they were the eldest male child. However, from 1300–1922, there was an empire based in eastern Europe and western Asia known as the Ottoman Empire. When the Ottoman sultan died, his sons had to fight each other before one could take control of the empire. The victorious one then killed the others. This system continued until 1603, when the eldest son succeeded his father automatically.

The oldest monarchy in the world is in Japan. The imperial line is said to date back 2,600 years to the first emperor, who was a descendant of the Sun goddess. Japanese emperors were believed to be gods, but much of the real power in Japan belonged to military rulers, known as **shoguns**.

Emperor Akihito (center) is the current emperor of Japan.

14

The Incas lived in Peru in South America in the 1400s. Like the Japanese, the Incas believed that their rulers were descended from the Sun. Because their empire was so vast, Inca emperors sent their most powerful nobles to govern distant parts of the empire on their behalf.

Pachacutec was a military hero who expanded the Inca Empire. He was made ruler in 1438.

Today, we are used to women holding positions of power. Four hundred and fifty years ago, this was almost unheard of. Elizabeth I was the exception to this rule. She was only twenty-five when she became queen of England in 1558, but she proved to be one of the strongest and most influential monarchs England has ever had.

From 1547, Russia's rulers were called tsars. They had complete power and were known for their ambition and ruthlessness. Ivan IV became known as Ivan the Terrible because he killed so many people.

Elizabeth I of England

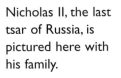

Nicholas II, the last tsar of Russia, is pictured here with his family.

Types of Government Today

There are many forms of government in the world today. The most common is democracy. Here is a chart of some of the main types of government.

Type	Description	Examples
Democracy		
Parliamentary Democracy	Elected representatives sit in parliament and form a government. Includes parliamentary republics and constitutional monarchies.	Australia, Canada, Germany, New Zealand, Republic of Ireland, Spain, United Kingdom
Presidential Republic	Citizens directly elect a national leader called a **president**.	Brazil, France, Russia, South Africa, United States
Alternative Forms of Government		
Communist State	Property and business is owned by the government.	Cuba, People's Republic of China
Theocracy	Power is held by religious leaders.	Iran, Vatican City
Monarchy	Power is held by the ruling monarch.	Brunei, Jordan, Oman, Saudi Arabia
Military Government	Power is seized and held by military leaders.	Myanmar (Burma), Sudan
Dictatorship	A country ruled by a leader with absolute, or total, power.	Libya

Democracy

Most countries in the world are democracies. Their citizens have a major role in electing the government and deciding what decisions the government can make on their behalf. Governing a country is a complex business, with many difficult decisions to be made every day. Citizens cannot be consulted on every issue, so they must let their governments act on their behalf. Each country has developed its own style of democracy. The two main types of democracy are parliamentary democracy and presidential republic.

U.S. Declaration of Independence

In 1994, Nelson Mandela became the first democratically elected president of South Africa.

In 1984, voters celebrated the first democratic elections in Brazil for twenty-five years.

A Haitian distributes election material for a presidential candidate.

Albanian graffiti calling for democracy in 1992.

Parliamentary Democracy

Many countries in the world, including the United Kingdom, Canada, Australia, and most of Europe, are parliamentary democracies. In these countries, power lies with **parliament**, which is made up of people elected from all regions of the country. The people elected to parliament are called members. Members of parliament usually belong to a political party; the largest party in parliament forms the government and its leader becomes **prime minister**, or **head of government**.

In a parliamentary democracy, the **head of state** is not a member of any political party. He or she acts as a figurehead, or symbol of the nation. The head of state can be either a monarch (as in the United Kingdom and Spain) or a president elected by parliament (as in Germany) or elected directly by the people (as in Ireland).

The United Kingdom's monarch, Elizabeth II (center), poses with other reigning European sovereigns.

Australian Prime Minister Julia Gillard shakes hands with UN Secretary-General Ban Ki-moon.

The parliament building in Budapest, Hungary, was built in the nineteenth century and is a major tourist site.

Presidential Republic

In a presidential republic, the head of state, or president, has real power. The president is elected either by the people, as in the United States, Russia, Mexico, or France, or by parliament as head of the largest political party, as in South Africa. In both cases, the president serves for a fixed period—usually four to six years—before he or she has to be elected again.

Supporters of Nelson Mandela campaigned for him to be elected president of South Africa in 1994.

Presidents usually have a great deal of power since they are the leaders of the nation. In the United States, the president runs the government. This means that he or she is responsible for seeing that all laws made by Congress are enforced. The president, however, does not make the laws. Congress is made up of people elected from each state. Sometimes, as in France, the president may appoint a prime minister to help. Presidents are often in charge of the armed services, manage the national finances, handle relations with foreign countries, and represent the country when traveling abroad.

American president Barack Obama was elected for a second term in 2013.

Alternative Forms of Government

Although democracy is the world's most common form of government, there are other ways of running a country. Here are five alternative types of governments.

Communist State

Communist governments, such as those in China and Cuba, are based on the idea that the country itself, not private individuals, should own property, industry, and business, so that everyone has an equal share of the nation's wealth. Because everyone is equal, everyone can be represented by one party, the communist party, which runs the country on their behalf.

Cuban leader,
Fidel Castro

Theocracy

A theocracy is a country ruled by religious leaders. Today, there are only two theocracies in the world: Islamic Iran and the Roman Catholic Vatican City, the headquarters of the pope in Rome.

Ayatollah Ali Khameni,
leader of Iran

Monarchy

In the past, every monarch was the absolute, or total, ruler of a country and had complete power over his or her subjects. Most monarchs have now handed over their powers to parliament and have no real power, as in the United Kingdom. Some, as in Saudi Arabia, Brunei, and Swaziland in southern Africa, still have enough power to govern their countries as they see fit.

Sultan of Brunei

Military Government

When a monarch or an elected government fails to govern properly, the armed services may intervene and run the country themselves. Although military leaders are very good at keeping order, they are not usually as good at running a country. Many military governments eventually hand their powers back to an elected government.

Dictatorship

Some countries are run by a **dictator**, a single, usually unelected ruler who holds total power. Dictators may have advisors to rely on but will always have the final say themselves. Dictators control the armed services and the police, so they are able to keep every citizen under control. They usually do not allow political parties, so no one can organize against them. They also control schools, television, and newspapers, so people learn only what is acceptable to the dictator.

the army of Myanmar (Burma) on parade

How Governments Are Chosen

In a democracy, the people who have been elected have to be re-elected or new people must be elected within a certain number of years. However, the leaders of countries that are not democratic change in other ways.

When a government is run by a non-democratic ruler, such as a monarch, it changes when one leader—the monarch—dies and his or her successor takes over. With a military government, the leader changes when one military leader replaces another. In both cases, the people of the country have no choice as to what their new government will be like or who will serve in it. In a democratic nation, however, that choice lies with the people, who make their decisions through voting in **elections**. If all adult men and women in a country are allowed to vote, this is known as universal suffrage.

Female Suffrage

Until about 100 years ago, suffrage, or the right to vote, was limited to men—and only wealthy men. No women could vote, as they were not considered equal to men. All that changed in 1869, when women in the state of Wyoming gained the vote. In 1893, New Zealand became the first country to have universal suffrage. All women in the United States gained the vote for the first time in 1920. British women did not get equal voting rights with men until 1928.

Kate Sheppard (1847–1934), New Zealand suffragette

Elections

An election is when every eligible citizen of a country has the opportunity to vote for the candidate of their choice to form a new government. In most countries, every man and woman over a specific age can vote. The minimum age ranges from sixteen to twenty-one. In a few countries, such as Saudi Arabia, women still do not have the right to vote.

These citizens in Jakarta, Indonesia, supported Megawati Sukarnoputri in the presidential elections.

In a democratic nation, such as the United States, **voters** have two or more candidates to choose from. Each candidate describes his or her plans for the government. Voters learn what the candidates' ideas are on important issues, such as education or public transportation. Then they can choose the person they think will do the best job at running the government.

Silvio Berlusconi celebrated becoming president of Italy in 2001.

Candidates work hard to gain enough votes to win. They visit different places to meet voters. They make public speeches. In some countries, they or their parties may advertise in newspapers and on television.

Posters are a popular way of trying to win votes.

Voting

On election day, every voter has the chance, and the responsibility, to vote. Some people mail in their vote, but most go to their local polling place to vote. In many countries, voting machines are used. Telephones, the Internet, and even cell phones are sometimes used to help people vote more easily.

After everyone has voted, the votes are counted and the results declared. One main way of counting votes and arriving at a decision is known as a simple majority. In this method, voters mark their choice. The candidate with the largest number of votes wins, even if this is less than half the total.

An electronic voting system was used in India in 1999.

Archbishop Desmond Tutu votes in the South African elections in 2009.

In some countries, such as the United States, citizens vote for the president and members of Congress individually. This means that the head of the government and the members of the lawmaking branch of the government are often from different political groups, or parties. Political groups are a collection of people who have similar goals about how to run the country. In this system, people with different ideas have to find a way to work together so that the interests of many groups are represented.

In other countries, such as the United Kingdom, the largest political party in government runs the country. The other political parties form the opposition to it, and offer constructive criticism to the government to make sure that other interests are heard.

How Often Do Leaders Change?

Democracies hold elections at different intervals. Most countries have elections every two to six years, with the gap between each election either fixed or set at a maximum time. In the United Kingdom, an election for parliament must happen at least every five years. In the United States, the president is elected for four years and may be elected a second time. If the president is convicted of a crime by the Congress, he or she is removed from office.

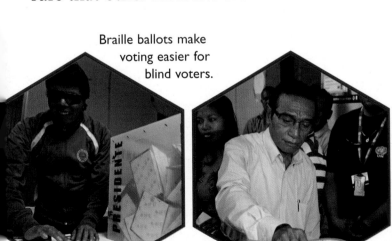

Braille ballots make voting easier for blind voters.

Citizens in East Timor voted in the country's first independent elections in 1999.

Changing the Government

In democracies, governments change as people's needs and desires change. Most democracies have fair and frequent elections and regularly updated laws, which adjust to the changing conditions of the world.

Many countries have **constitutions** that describe how the government can be changed and even how to change the constitution. For example, the U.S. Constitution includes a section that tells how amendments, or new sections, can be made in order to change or expand the Constitution.

Not all governments are able to change as smoothly. Some are changed by **revolutions**, or uprisings. One group of people, or a political party within a country, may feel that the current government isn't working well. It may believe it knows a better way to run the country. If enough people feel the same way, they may be able to overthrow the government and take control. Sometimes revolutions can be long and difficult, and many people lose their property and often risk their lives.

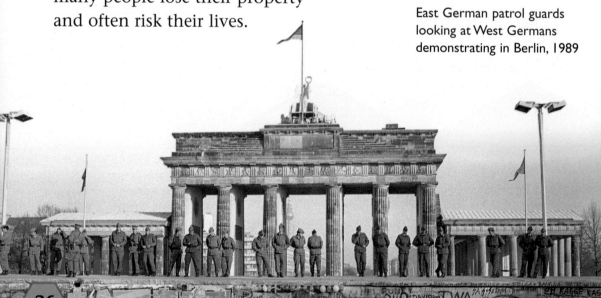

East German patrol guards looking at West Germans demonstrating in Berlin, 1989

Almost every country in the world has had a revolution at least once in its history. In the 1640s, England had a revolution that led to the execution of the king, Charles I, and the setting up of a republic that lasted for eleven years. The United States came into existence when the thirteen colonies revolted against British rule and declared independence in 1776. France had a major revolution beginning in 1789.

Mexican revolutionaries posing with guns drawn in 1916

One of the most important revolutions in world history occurred in Russia in 1917. At that time, Russia was at war with Germany and there was a severe shortage of both food and coal. Tsar Nicholas II was an absolute monarch, and his government was not popular. When workers went on strike in March 1917, the tsar's soldiers refused to support him. The tsar abdicated, or resigned, and a new government was formed. This government also had problems, and in November 1917, a second revolution led to the creation of the world's first communist government.

Communists in Moscow, Russia, during the revolution in 1917

What's Your Role?

Writing letters to your political representative is one way of making your voice heard.

Everybody in a democracy has the right to play a role in government, even if they cannot vote, and that includes you! You can make your voice heard, whether you agree with the government or not, in many different ways.

You can let the government know your opinions by writing letters to your elected leaders or to the newspapers. If you want to talk to more people you can try to get interviewed by a radio or television station. You can also go to your local leaders and explain your feelings.

When you are old enough, you may want to run for a political position and have your say directly. In the meantime, you can practice being politically active by joining school committees or participating in school elections.

British Prime Minister Tony Blair meets with an association for disabled schoolchildren.

You might feel very strongly about an issue. You could get together with others to petition, or ask for, a change to a law or ask the government to change a particular **policy**. The more people you get to sign the petition, the more likely the government will be to listen to your point of view.

By taking advantage of your democratic right to vote, to protest, and to make your opinions known peacefully, you can help improve your government and improve the future of your town, local community, or country.

In 2003, Italian demonstrators held a rally to protest against war in Iraq.

In 1998, Indonesian students staged a peaceful occupation of parliament and demanded the resignation of President Suharno.

Glossary

citizens   members of a country

communist   a political system in which property and business are owned by the government, not by individuals

constitutions   the basic laws and plans that explain how a government is organized and run

currency   paper money and coins used in a country to purchase goods and services

democracy   a system of government in which citizens take part in the decision-making process

dictator   a ruler who holds complete, or absolute, power

elections   the selections (by vote) of candidates for political office, such as a president or member of parliament or Congress

head of government   the political leader of the government, such as a prime minister, who serves under the head of state

head of state   the leader of a country, such as a president or monarch

monarchy   a country headed by a king, queen, tsar, or sultan

parliament   an elected group of people who gather together to discuss public issues and make laws

policy   plan of action adopted or pursued by a government, politician, or political party

president   the head of state and elected leader of a republic

prime minister   the head of government in a parliamentary democracy, such as a monarchy or republic

republic   a country headed by an elected leader who is not a monarch

revolutions   the overthrow or change, often violent, of one type of government for another

shoguns   military commanders in Japanese history

voters   citizens who are eligible to vote in an election

Index